FUNNY
MONEY

Other humorous quotation books by Prion:

Des MacHale
Wit
Wit Hits The Spot
Wit On Target
Wit – The Last Laugh
Wit Rides Again
Ultimate Wit
Ready Wit
Irish Wit

Michelle Lovric
Women's Wicked Wit
More Women's Wicked Wit

Rosemarie Jarski
Hollywood Wit
Wisecracks

Michael Powell
High Society

FUNNY MONEY

Priceless Quotations from Billionaires to Bankrupts

Michael Powell

PRION

First published 2004 in Great Britain by

Prion
an imprint of the
Carlton Publishing Group
20 Mortimer Street
London W1T 3JW

ISBN 1-85375-503-6

Printed in Great Britain
by Mackays

CONTENTS

Arts

The opera always loses money. That is as it should be. Opera has no business making money.

New York Times

Religion and art spring from the same root and are close kin. Economics and art are strangers.

Willa Cather

If you want to get rich from writing, write the sort of thing that's read by persons who move their lips when they're reading to themselves.

Don Marquis

As soon as any art is pursued with a view of
money, then farewell, in ninety-nine cases out of
a hundred, all hope of genuine good work.

Samuel Butler

I'm afraid, Mr Goldwyn, that we shall not ever
be able to do business together. You see, you're
an artist, and care only about art, while I'm only
a tradesman and care only about money.

George Bernard Shaw

Being good in business is the most fascinating
kind of art ... Making money is art and
working is art and good business is the best art.

Andy Warhol

Most idealistic people are skint. I have
discovered that people with money have no
imagination, and people with imagination have
no money.

George Weiss

You cannot combine the pursuit of money with the pursuit of art.

George Bernard Shaw

Half of the large sum paid me for writing a movie script was in payment for listening to the producer and obeying him ... The movies pay as much for obedience as for creative work.

Ben Hecht

I went into the business for the money, and the art grew out of it. If people are disillusioned by that remark, I can't help it. It's the truth.

Charlie Chaplin

Writing is turning one's worst moments into money.

J. P. Donleavy

Bankruptcy

Bankruptcy stared me in the face, but one thought kept me calm; soon I'd be too poor to need an anti-theft alarm.

Gina Rothfels

Capitalism without bankruptcy is like Christianity without hell.

Frank Borman, CEO, Eastern Airlines

A nation is not in danger of financial disaster merely because it owes itself money.

Andrew Mellon

Most people become bankrupt through having invested too heavily in the prose of life.

Oscar Wilde

It is said that the world is in a state of bankruptcy, that the world owes the world more than the world can pay.

Ralph Waldo Emerson

Bankruptcy is a legal proceeding in which you put your money in your pants pocket and give your coat to your creditors.

Joey Adams

Banks and
Bankers

A financier is a pawn-broker with imagination.

Arthur Wing Pinero

Blaming the World Bank for poverty is a bit like
blaming the Red Cross for starting World Wars
I and II.

Michael Moore

Banking may well be a career from which no
man really recovers.

John Kenneth Galbraith

I work for an investment bank. I have dealt with code written by stock exchanges. I have seen how the computer systems that store your money are run. If I ever make a fortune, I will store it in gold bullion under my bed.

Matthew Crosby

Over a long weekend I could teach my dog to be an investment banker.

Herbert A. Allen

Why do banks use all that space and money to construct so many teller stations, then never have more than two or three in use?

Justin A. Ward

It is a rather pleasant experience to be alone in a bank at night.

Willie Sutton

Bank failures are caused by depositors who don't deposit enough money to cover losses due to mismanagement.

Dan Quayle

What you said hurt me very much. I cried all the way to the bank.

Liberace

Except for con men borrowing money they shouldn't get and the widows who have to visit with the handsome young men in the trust department, no sane person ever enjoyed visiting a bank.

Martin Mayer

If you owe the bank one hundred dollars, that's your problem. If you owe the bank one hundred million dollars, that's the bank's problem.

John Paul Getty

A bank is a place where they lend you an umbrella in fair weather and ask for it back when it begins to rain.

Robert Frost

For a country, everything will be lost when the jobs of an economist and a banker become highly respected professions.

Montesquieu

What is robbing a bank compared with founding a bank?

Bertolt Brecht, *The Threepenny Opera*

With a group of bankers I always had the feeling that success was measured by the extent one gave nothing away.

Lord Longford

The process by which banks create money is so simple that the mind is repelled.

John Kenneth Galbraith

History records that the money changers have used every form of abuse, intrigue, deceit, and violent means possible to maintain their control over governments by controlling money and its issuance.

James Madison

I went to the bank and asked to borrow a cup of money. They said, 'What for?' I said, 'I'm going to buy some sugar.'

Steven Wright

Bankers are just like everyone else only richer.

Ogden Nash

Because bankers measure their self-worth in money, and pay themselves a lot of it, they think they're fine fellows and don't need to explain themselves.

James Buchan

I hesitate to deposit money in a bank. I am afraid I shall never dare to take it out again. When you go to confession and entrust your sins to the safe-keeping of the priest, do you ever come back for them?

Jean Baudrillard

The recovery in profitability has been amazing ... leaving Barings to conclude that it was not actually terribly difficult to make money in the securities business.

Peter Baring, Chairman of Barings Bank

A bank is a place that will lend you money if you can prove that you don't need it.

Bob Hope

I hate banks. They do nothing positive for anybody except take care of themselves. They're first in with their fees and first out when there's trouble.

Harvey Goldsmith

The rest of the market had smelled what Barings back in London were completely ignoring: that I was in so deep there was no way out.

Nick Leeson

The private control of credit is the modern form of slavery.

Upton Sinclair

When a banker jumps out of a window, jump after him – that's where the money is.

Robespierre

Business

I'm a chartered accountant; but please when you go home not a word to my parents; they think I'm playing the piano in a brothel.

Bruce Marshall, *The Bank Audit*

I thought there would be a few raised eyebrows when I applied for the money, but the grant was approved.

Frank Turner, on receiving a grant of £22,000 from his local council to renovate his sex shop

When money is at stake, never be the first to mention sums.

Sheikh Ahmed Yamani, former Saudi Arabian Oil Minister

Business is the art of extracting money from another man's pocket without resorting to violence.

Max Amsterdam

Human capital has replaced dollar capital.

Michael Milken

A federal judge has ruled that Microsoft should be split into two different companies. One company will have the Windows operating system and the other will count Bill Gates's money.

Conan O'Brien

It sounds extraordinary but it's a fact that balance sheets can make fascinating reading.

Mary Archer

A business that makes nothing but money is a poor business.

Henry Ford

Business ethics is to ethics as Monopoly money
is to money.

Harold Hendersen

Business? It's quite simple: it's other people's
money.

Alexandre Dumas

In the business world, everyone is paid in two
coins: cash and experience. Take the experience
first; the cash will come later.

Harold S. Geneen

What is high finance? It's knowing the
difference between one and ten, multiplying,
subtracting and adding. You just add noughts.
It's no more than that.

John Bentley

There is only one boss. The customer. And he can fire everybody in the company from the chairman on down, simply by spending his money somewhere else.

Sam Walton

The TV business ... is a cruel and shallow money trench, a long plastic hallway where thieves and pimps run free and good men die like dogs. There's also a negative side.

Hunter S. Thompson

Catch a man a fish, and you can sell it to him. Teach a man to fish, and you ruin a wonderful business opportunity.

Karl Marx

Every sale has five basic obstacles: no need, no money, no hurry, no desire, no trust.

Zig Ziglar

It is unfortunate we can't buy many business executives for what they are worth and sell them for what they think they are worth.

Malcolm Forbes

There's no business like show business, but there are several businesses like accounting.

David Letterman

If you bet on a horse, that's gambling. If you bet you can make three spades, that's entertainment. If you bet cotton will go up three points, that's business. See the difference?

William Sherrod

I'm probably the worst businessman known to man because I never wanted to make money.

Tony Wilson

Humans must breathe, but corporations must make money.

Alice Embree

Capitalism and Communism

Marxism is essentially a product of the
bourgeois mind.

Joseph A. Schumpeter

The financial policy of the welfare state requires
that there be no way for the owners of wealth to
protect themselves.

Alan Greenspan

In a consumer society, there are inevitably two
kinds of slaves: the prisoners of addiction and
the prisoners of envy.

Ivan Illich

All social rules and all relations between individuals are eroded by a cash economy, avarice drags Pluto himself out of the bowels of the earth.

Karl Marx

Capital is a result of labour, and is used by labour to assist it in further production. Labour is the active and initial force, and labour is therefore the employer of capital.

Henry George

Economic progress, in capitalist society, means turmoil.

Joseph A. Schumpeter

As soon as the land of any country has all become private property, the landlords, like all other men, love to reap where they never sowed.

Adam Smith

The evolution of the capitalist style of life could be easily – and perhaps most tellingly – described in terms of the genesis of the modern Lounge Suit.

Joseph A. Schumpeter

There is only one way to kill capitalism – by taxes, taxes, and more taxes.

Karl Marx

We have two economic systems working for America: capitalism for the rich and socialism for the poor. The problem with a government that lets both systems operate is that the middle class gets stuck working for the rich to support the poor.

Star Parker

The market came with the dawn of civilisation and it is not an invention of capitalism … If it leads to improving the well-being of the people there is no contradiction with socialism.

Mikhail Gorbachev

If you want to see the acceptable face of capitalism, go out to an oil rig in the North Sea.

Edward Heath

When I gave food to the poor, they called me a saint. When I asked why the poor were hungry, they called me a communist.

Dom H. Camara

In the 1980s capitalism triumphed over communism. In the 1990s it triumphed over democracy.

David Korten

Capitalism is what people do if you leave them alone.

Kenneth Minogue

The forces in a capitalist society, if left unchecked, tend to make the rich richer and the poor poorer.

Jawaharlal Nehru

Fascism should more appropriately be called corporatism because it is a merger of state and corporate power.

Benito Mussolini

Thank God we're a capitalist society and there's nothing wrong with running after money.

Roger Tamraz

If you want to destroy capitalism and the society that goes with it, you must begin by debauching the currency.

Lenin

Under capitalism, man exploits man. Under communism, it's just the opposite.

John Kenneth Galbraith

The intermediate stage between socialism and capitalism is alcoholism.

Norman Brenner

What breaks capitalism, all that will ever break capitalism, is capitalists. The faster they run the more strain on their heart.

Raymond Williams

It is hypocritical for feminists and intellectuals to enjoy the pleasures and conveniences of capitalism while sneering at it … Everyone born into capitalism has incurred a debt to it. Give Caesar his due.

Camille Paglia

People say, 'You get what you pay for', but that can't be true if capitalism is to succeed.

Eli Khamarov

Capitalism needs to function like a game of tug-of-war. Two opposing sides need to continually struggle for dominance, but at no time can either side be permitted to walk away with the rope.

Pete Holiday

The first rule of venture capitalism should be
Shoot the Inventor.

Sir Richard Storey

[Capitalism is] that commercial system in which
supply immediately answers to demand, and in
which everybody seems to be thoroughly
dissatisfied and unable to get anything he wants.

G. K. Chesterton

If capitalism works, why are there so many
stupid rich people?

Anon

Only when the last tree has been felled, the last
river poisoned and the last fish caught, man will
know that he cannot eat money.

American Indian wisdom

Making capitalism out of socialism is like
making eggs out of an omelette.

Vadim Bakatin

Capital is money, capital is commodities ... By virtue of it being value, it has acquired the occult ability to add value to itself. It brings forth living offspring, or, at the least, lays golden eggs.

Karl Marx

Money is the barometer of a society's virtue.

Ayn Rand

The inherent vice of capitalism is the unequal sharing of blessings; the inherent virtue of socialism is the equal sharing of miseries.

Winston Churchill

The system of corporate life is a new power for which our language contains no name. We have no word to express government by moneyed corporations.

Charles Francis Adams

Capital is dead labour that, vampire-like, lives only by sucking living labour, and lives the more the more labour that it sucks.

Karl Marx

And what does the money machine eat to shit out? It eats youth, spontaneity, life, beauty and above all it eats creativity. It eats quality and shits out quantity.

William Burroughs

Communism doesn't work because people like to own stuff.

Frank Zappa

Capitalism is the astounding belief that the most wickedest of men will do the most wickedest of things for the greatest good of everyone.

John Maynard Keynes

Nothing can have value without being an object of utility.

Karl Marx

Capitalism is using its money; we socialists throw it away.

Fidel Castro

Charity

Give us your f**king money.

Bob Geldof, Live Aid, 1985

A 'government subsidy' is getting just some of your own money back.

Metzger's Maxim

The poor don't know that their function in life is to exercise our generosity.

Jean-Paul Sartre

People think that if they were rich they would contribute to charities. My experience has been that if you don't start giving away your money when you have very little, you won't do it when you get a lot.

Robert Bainum

A foundation is a large body of money completely surrounded by people who want some.

Dwight MacDonald

It is every man's obligation to put back into the world at least the equivalent of what he takes out of it.

Albert Einstein

Don't offer me advice; give me money.

Spanish proverb

WORK HARDER! ... Millions on welfare depend on YOU!!!

Bumper sticker

37

When the rich assemble to concern themselves
with the business of the poor it is called charity.
When the poor assemble to concern themselves
with the business of the rich it is called
anarchy.

Paul Richard

Definition of 'foreign aid': the transfer of money
from poor people in rich countries to rich
people in poor countries.

Anon

We still have to find some way of combining
Christian charity with sensible social policy.

Margaret Thatcher

I spent my whole life working for charity, now I
work for money. It's just as much fun.

Charlotte Ford

Charity creates a multitude of sins.

Oscar Wilde

Charity is injurious unless it helps the recipient to become independent of it.

> John D. Rockefeller

When I have money, I get rid of it quickly, lest it find a way into my heart.

> John Wesley

Feeding the starving poor only increases their number.

> Benjamin Bova

We're a sentimental people. We like a few kind words better than millions of dollars given in a humiliating way.

> Gamal Abdel Nasser on refusing
> Western economic assistance, 1969

The more is given the less people will work for themselves, and the less they work the more their poverty will increase.

> Leo Tolstoy

The best investment I know of is charity: you get your principal back immediately, and draw a dividend every time you think of it.

Josh Billings

Charity, as if it didn't have enough trouble in this day and age, will always be suspected of morbidity, sado-masochism, perversity of some sort. All higher or moral tendencies lie under suspicion of being rackets.

Saul Bellow

Don't use the impudence of a beggar as an excuse for not helping him.

Rabbi Schmelke of Nicolsburg

Philanthropy is commendable, but it must not cause the philanthropist to overlook the circumstances of economic injustice which make philanthropy necessary.

Martin Luther King, Jr

I try to give to the poor people for love what the rich could get for money. No, I wouldn't touch a leper for a thousand pounds; yet I willingly cure him for the love of God.

Mother Teresa

Charity begins at home, and generally dies from lack of outdoor exercise.

Anon

Sir, he throws away his money without thought and without merit. I do not call a tree generous that sheds its fruit at every breeze.

Samuel Johnson

Posthumous charities are the very essence of selfishness, when bequeathed by those who, when alive, would part with nothing.

Charles Caleb Colton

41

We'd all like a reputation for generosity, and we'd all like to buy it cheap.

Mignon McLaughlin

One must be poor to know the luxury of giving!

George Eliot

Philanthropist: a rich old gentleman who has trained himself to grin while his conscience is picking his pocket.

Ambrose Bierce

Charity sees the need, not the cause.

German proverb

We are all here on earth to help others; what on earth the others are here for I don't know.

W. H. Auden

We are for aiding our allies by sharing some of our material blessings with those nations which share in our fundamental beliefs ... We bought dress suits for Greek undertakers, extra wives for Kenyan government officials. We bought a thousand TV sets for a place where they have no electricity.

Ronald Reagan

Never give money to a preacher who has a better car than you do.

Anon

Anticipate charity by preventing poverty.

Maimonides

Money is like manure. You have to spread it around or it smells.

John Paul Getty

43

Children

The only wealth in this world is children, more than all the money and power on earth.

Mario Puzo, *The Godfather III*

Children are rarely in the position to lend one a truly interesting sum of money. There are, however, exceptions, and such children are an excellent addition to any party.

Fran Lebowitz

If I were a Brazilian without land or money or the means to feed my children, I would be burning the rain forest too.

Sting

A lot of pop music is about stealing pocket money from children.

Ian Anderson

In bringing up children, spend on them half as much money and twice as much time.

Anon

Children are a poor man's riches.

English proverb

No matter how bad a child is, he is still good for a tax deduction.

American proverb

Adults are just children who earn money.

Kenneth Brannagh

If it weren't for baseball, many kids wouldn't know what a millionaire looked like.

Phyllis Diller

Class

There is only one class in the community that thinks more about money than the rich, and that is the poor. The poor can think of nothing else.

Oscar Wilde

The genius of our ruling class is that it has kept a majority of the people from ever questioning the inequity of a system where most people drudge along, paying heavy taxes for which they get nothing in return.

Gore Vidal

The fundamental class division in any society is not between rich and poor, or between farmers and city dwellers, but between taxpayers and tax consumers.

David Boaz

Of all classes the rich are the most noticed and the least studied.

John Kenneth Galbraith

Wearing overalls on weekdays, painting somebody else's house to earn money? You're working class. Wearing overalls at weekends, painting your own house to save money? You're middle class.

Lawrence Sutton

Nowadays, people can be divided into three classes – the Haves, the Have-Nots, and the Have-Not-Paid-for-What-They-Haves.

Earl Wilson

Crime and Corruption

He without benefit of scruples
His fun and money soon quadruples.

Ogden Nash

You can fool all of the people all of the time if the advertising is right and the budget is big enough.

Joseph E. Levine

They had been corrupted by money, and he had been corrupted by sentiment. Sentiment was the more dangerous, because you couldn't name its price.

Graham Greene, *The Heart of the Matter*

Those who steal from private individuals spend their lives in stocks and chains; those who steal from the public treasure go dressed in gold and purple.

Marcius Porcius Cato

Everything and everyone can be bought and sold, and government is irrelevant.

Marc Rich

The difference between tax avoidance and tax evasion is the thickness of a prison wall.

Denis Healey

The surest way to remain poor is to be an honest man.

Napoleon Bonaparte

Nearly all desires of the poor are punished by prison.

Louis-Ferdinand Céline

No one can earn a million dollars honestly.

William Jennings Bryan

The advent of electronic transfers, capable of winging millions across the world in a blink of an eye, means that dirty money can wing its way through half a dozen countries and twice as many different accounts before the police can pull their boots on.

Jeremy Scott-Joynt

Nothing is illegal if one hundred businessmen decide to do it.

Andrew Young

I wouldn't be in a legitimate business for all the … money in the world.

Gennaro Anguilo, Boston organised crime boss

Beauty provoketh thieves sooner than gold.

William Shakespeare, *As You Like It*

There are only three ways to deal with a blackmailer. You can pay him and pay him and pay him until you're penniless. Or you can call the police yourself and let your secret be known to the world. Or you can kill him.

Edward de Bono, *The Woman in the Window*

A lawyer with his briefcase can steal more than a hundred men with guns.

Mario Puzo

The law is bigger than money – but only if the law works hard enough.

Thomas E. Dewey

Under the rules of a society that cannot distinguish between profit and profiteering, between money defined as necessity and money defined as luxury, murder is occasionally obligatory and always permissible.

Lewis H. Lapham

He must have killed a lot of men to have made
so much money.

Molière, *Le Malade Imaginaire*

Whenever we needed money, we robbed the
airport. To us it was better than Citibank.

Henry Hill, *GoodFellas*

A counterfeiter is the only man whose wife
never complains that he doesn't make enough
money.

Anon

No matter what crimes a man may have
committed or how cynically he may have
debased his talent or his friends, variations on
the answer, 'Yes, but I did it for the money',
satisfy all but the most tiresome objections.

Lewis H. Lapham

Behind every great fortune there is a crime.

Honoré de Balzac

I rob banks because that's where the money is.

Willie Sutton

Organised crime in America takes in over $40 billion a year and spends very little on office supplies.

Woody Allen

If he survived that jump with a plastic parachute, he deserves to keep all the money he stole because that would be the miracle of the century.

Philippine Airlines spokesman on the hijacker who robbed passengers at gunpoint and escaped by leaping out of the plane with a homemade parachute

Death

On September 11th the imaginary wall that divided the rich world from the poor world came crashing down.

James Wolfensohn, President, World Bank

Early to rise and early to bed makes a male healthy and wealthy and dead.

James Thurber

I'm spending a year dead for tax reasons.

Douglas Adams

I don't want to tell you how much insurance I carry with the Prudential, but all I can say is: when I go, they go too.

Jack Benny

There's no reason to be the richest man in the cemetery. You can't do any business from there.

Colonel Sanders

I've got all the money I'll ever need if I die by four o'clock this afternoon.

Henny Youngman

The wages of sin are death, but by the time taxes are taken out, it's just sort of a tired feeling.

Paula Poundstone

I hope that after I die, people will say of me: 'That guy sure owed me a lot of money.'

Jack Handey

Pale death knocks with impartial foot at poor men's hovels and king's palaces.

Horace

By the time I have money to burn, my fire will have burnt out.

Anon

The pride of dying rich raises the loudest laugh in hell.

John Foster

He that dies pays all debts.

William Shakespeare, *The Tempest*

He neither drank, smoked, nor rode a bicycle. Living frugally, saving his money, he died early, surrounded by greedy relatives. It was a great lesson to me.

John Barrymore

Debt and Credit

Money was invented so we could know exactly how much we owe.

Cullen Hightower

It's better to give than to lend and it costs about the same.

Philip Gibbs

I can get no remedy against this consumption of the purse: borrowing only lingers and lingers it out, but the disease is incurable.

William Shakespeare, *Henry IV, Part 2*

It's always struck me how the government gives
money to people not in work, then only gives
students loans that are worth less than benefits
when they are working hard.

Gavin Merrifield, Student

One must have some sort of occupation
nowadays. If I hadn't my debts I shouldn't have
anything to think about.

Oscar Wilde, *A Woman of No Importance*

Money can't buy everything. That's what credit
cards are for.

Anon

I'm not the man I used to be, so why should I
have to pay off his debts?

Gary Apple

Credit cards have three dimensions: height,
width and debt.

Shelby Friedman

The creditor hath a better memory than the debtor.

James Howell

Those who despise money will eventually sponge off their friends.

Chinese proverb

Anyone who lives within his means suffers from a lack of imagination.

Lionel Stander

Modern man drives a mortgaged car over a bond-financed highway on credit-card gas.

Earl Wilson

Some debts are fun when you are acquiring them, but none are fun when you set about retiring them.

Ogden Nash

A small debt produces a debtor; a large one, an enemy.

Publilius Syrus

Solvency is maintained by means of a national debt, on the principle, 'If you will not lend me the money, how can I pay you?'

Ralph Waldo Emerson

It is only the poor who pay cash, and that not from virtue, but because they are refused credit.

Anatole France

Debt is the slavery of the free.

Publilius Syrus

Run for your life from any man who tells you that money is evil. That sentence is the leper's bell of an approaching looter.

Ayn Rand

Isn't it a shame that future generations can't be here to see all the wonderful things we're doing with their money?

Earl Wilson

If you don't have some bad loans you are not in business.

Paul Volcker

The surest way to get rid of a bore is to lend money to him.

Paul Louis Courier

Before borrowing money from a friend, decide which you need more.

Addison H. Hallock

Running into debt isn't so bad. It's running into creditors that hurts.

Anon

61

The human species, according to the best theory
I can form of it, is composed of two distinct
races, the men who borrow and the men who
lend.

Charles Lamb

Of course I'm doing something about my
overdraft: I'm seeing my accountant.

Barry Fantoni

Speak not of my debts unless you mean to pay
them.

George Herbert

Neither a borrower nor a lender be,
For loan oft loses both itself and friend,
And borrowing dulls the edge of husbandry.

William Shakespeare, *Hamlet*

The surest way to establish your credit is to work
yourself into the position of not needing any.

Maurice Switzer

Some people use one half their ingenuity to get into debt, and the other half to avoid paying it.

George D. Prentice

Home life ceases to be free and beautiful as soon as it is founded on borrowing and debt.

Henrik Ibsen, *A Doll's House*

Most people ... find a disorientating mismatch between the long-term nature of their liabilities and the increasingly short-term nature of their assets.

Howard Davies

Never spend your money before you have it.

Thomas Jefferson

We often pay our debts not because it is only fair that we should, but to make future loans easier.

François Duc de La Rochefoucauld

Blessed are the young, for they shall inherit the national debt.

Herbert Hoover

If there is anyone to whom I owe money, I'm prepared to forget it if they are.

Errol Flynn

The 1980s are to debt what the 1960s were to sex. The 1960s left a hangover. So will the 1980s.

James Grant

I'm living so far beyond my income that we may almost be said to be living apart.

e e cummings

The only reason I made a commercial for American Express was to pay for my American Express bill.

Peter Ustinov

Everybody likes a kidder, but nobody lends him money.

Arthur Miller

Economics

I guess I should warn you, if I turn out to be particularly clear, you've probably misunderstood what I've said.

Alan Greenspan, from a speech to the Economic Club of New York, 1988

Economics is war pursued by other means.

Raymond F. DeVoe, Jr

All the perplexities, confusion and distress in America rise ... from downright ignorance of the nature of coin, credit and circulation.

John Adams, in a letter to Thomas Jefferson, 1787

The trouble with today's economy is that when a man is rich, it's all on paper. When he's broke, it's cash.

Sam Marconi

Economics is extremely useful as a form of employment for economists.

John Kenneth Galbraith

All the great economic ills the world has faced this century can be directly traced back to the London School of Economics.

N. M. Perrera

An economist is a man who states the obvious in terms of the incomprehensible.

Alfred A. Knopf

Did you ever think that making a speech on economics is a lot like pissing down your leg? It seems hot to you, but it never does to anyone else.

Lyndon B. Johnson

Unlimited economic growth has the marvellous quality of stilling discontent while maintaining privilege, a fact that has not gone unnoticed among liberal economists.

Noam Chomsky

Undermine the entire economic structure of society by leaving the pay toilet door ajar so the next person can get in free.

Taylor Meade

Economics is an entire scientific discipline of not knowing what you're talking about.

P. J. O'Rourke

An economist is an expert who will know tomorrow why the things he predicted yesterday didn't happen today.

Evan Esar

Most economic fallacies derive ... from the tendency to assume that there is a fixed pie, that one party can gain only at the expense of another.

Milton Friedman

Every year the international finance system kills more people than the Second World War. But at least Hitler was mad, you know.

Ken Livingstone

Money alone sets all the world in motion.

Publilius Syrus

In economics, the majority is always wrong.

John Kenneth Galbraith

Economists state their GNP growth projections to the nearest tenth of a percentage point to prove they have a sense of humour.

Edgar R. Fiedler

An accountant is a man hired to explain that you didn't make the money you did.

Anon

The entire economic system depends on the fact that people are willing to do unpleasant things in return for money.

Scott Adams

Economics is a subject that does not greatly respect one's wishes.

Nikita Khrushchev

An economist is someone who sees something working in practice and asks whether it would work in principle.

Stephen M. Goldfeld

Economists are people who work with money who lack the personality to be accountants.

Anon

Finance is the art of passing currency from hand to hand until it finally disappears.

Robert W. Sarnoff

If all economists were laid end to end, they would never reach a conclusion.

George Bernard Shaw

Money is always there but the pockets change; it is not in the same pockets after a change, and that is all there is to say about money.

Gertrude Stein

If you feed the horse enough oats, there'll always be something in the road for the sparrows.

John Kenneth Galbraith

The Euro

The economic benefit [of the euro] should be
clear and unambiguous.

Chancellor Gordon Brown, 1997

I believe that most housewives would rather pay
a little more than risk a bare cupboard ... It is
not a time for complacency ... It is not a time
to opt out of voting, nor to opt out of Europe.

Margaret Thatcher, *Daily Telegraph*, 1975

In my lifetime all the problems have come from
mainland Europe and all the solutions have
come from the English-speaking nations across
the world.

Margaret Thatcher, 1999

If we want to see our socialist policies implemented by the next Labour government, then a prerequisite for that and a central part of our manifesto must be a pledge to withdraw from Europe.

Jack Straw, 1980

By working with our partners in the EU, we can do what we were elected to do: re-enfranchise our people; and show them that their political choices matter.

Jack Straw, 2001

Above all, the EEC takes away Britain's freedom to follow the economic policies we need.

Tony Blair, Beaconsfield by-election leaflet, 1982

I fought to persuade my party to become a party of Europe ... I have no doubt at all that the future of my country lies in being at the heart of Europe.

Tony Blair, 1995

The Tories, more unitedly hostile to the single currency than ever before, now need above all to shift a growing public sense that the euro is somehow inevitable.

Andrew Marr talking about 'euro creep'

Flaunting It

They is some people who suddenly get loads of money who become very tasteless. How has you two managed to avoid that?

Ali G interviewing Posh and Becks for Comic Relief

I wasn't satisfied just to earn a good living. I was looking to make a statement.

Donald Trump

When a man is wealthy he may wear an old cloth.

Ghanaian proverb

Nouveau is better than no riche at all.

Monsieur Marc

Never dress down for the poor. They won't respect you for it. They want their First Lady to look like a million dollars.

Imelda Marcos

Whether he admits it or not, a man has been brought up to look at money as a sign of his virility, a symbol of his power, a bigger phallic symbol than a Porsche.

Victoria Billings

Some people think they are worth a lot of money just because they have it.

Fannie Hurst

The rule is not to talk about money with people who have much more or much less than you.

Katherine Whitehorn

Never keep up with the Joneses. Drag them down to your level. It's cheaper.

Quentin Crisp

Ostentation is the signal flag of hypocrisy.

Edwin Hubbel Chapin

A man who shows me his wealth is like a
beggar who shows me his poverty; they are
both looking for alms – the rich man for the
alms of my envy, the poor man for the alms of
my guilt.

Ben Hecht

Money doesn't talk, it swears.

Bob Dylan

I've learned something too: selling out is sweet
because you get to make a lot of money and
don't have to hang out with poor asses like you
guys. Screw you guys, I'm going home.

Eric Cartman, *South Park*

You mean you can actually spend $70,000 at
Woolworth's?

Bob Krasno after seeing Ike and Tina Turner's house

77

With the great part of rich people, the chief employment of riches consists in the parade of riches.

Adam Smith

Freedom

For me money has never had the sound of anything else but freedom.

Coco Chanel

I find all this money a considerable burden.

John Paul Getty

To be poor and independent is very nearly an impossibility.

William Cobbett

The only people who claim that money is not important are people who have enough money so that they are relieved of the ugly burden of thinking about it.

Joyce Carol Oates

Sometimes one pays most for the things one gets for nothing.

Albert Einstein

Poverty often deprives a man of all spirit and virtue; it is hard for an empty bag to stand upright.

Benjamin Franklin

I know at last what distinguishes man from animals: financial worries.

Romain Rolland

The American Dream is really money.

Jill Robinson

Money is power, freedom, a cushion, the root of all evil, the sum of blessings.

Carl Sandburg

Money ... enables us to get what we want instead of what other people think we want.

George Bernard Shaw

Freedom is the by-product of economic surplus.

Aneurin Bevan

What shall it profit a man, if he shall gain the whole world, and lose his own soul?

Mark 8:36

Money frees you from doing things you dislike. Since I dislike doing nearly everything, money is handy.

Groucho Marx

If a free society cannot help the many who are poor, it cannot save the few who are rich.

John F. Kennedy

Money is coined liberty, and so it is ten times dearer to a man who is deprived of freedom.

Fyodor Dostoevsky

A Negro has handicaps enough without having to pay taxes to support the education of white students to learn how to suppress him.

Charles Hamilton Houston (1895–1950), US lawyer

The most efficient labour-saving device is still money.

Franklin P. Jones

Gambling

The urge to gamble is so universal and its practice so pleasurable that I assume it must be evil.

Heywood Hale Broun

I figure you have the same chance of winning the lottery whether you play or not.

Fran Lebowitz

The difference between playing the stock market and the horses is that one of the horses must win.

Joey Adams

Casinos and prostitutes have the same thing in common; they are both trying to screw you out of your money and send you home with a smile on your face.

V. P. Pappy

There is no one quite as angry as someone who has just lost a lot of money.

David Williamson

I used to be a heavy gambler. But now I just make mental bets. That's how I lost my mind.

Steve Allen

The gambling known as business looks with austere disfavour upon the business known as gambling.

Ambrose Bierce

The rulers of the country generally believed that betting eliminates strikes. Men had to work in order to gamble.

Michael Ondaatje, *Running the Family*

There is in Hollywood, as in all cultures in which gambling is the central activity, a lowered sexual energy, an inability to devote more than token attention to the preoccupations of the society outside.

Joan Didion

No wife can endure a gambling husband unless he is a steady winner.

Lord Dewar

Certainly the game is rigged. Don't let that stop you; if you don't bet, you can't win.

Robert A. Heinlein

Slot machines sit there like young courtesans, promising pleasures undreamed of, your deepest desires fulfilled, all lusts satiated.

Frank Scoblete

Deep in the sea are riches beyond compare. But if you seek safety, it is on the shore.

Sheikh Saadi of Shiraz, *Rose Garden*

If I lose today, I can look forward to winning tomorrow, and if I win today, I can expect to lose tomorrow. A sure thing is no fun.

Chico Marx

You cannot beat a roulette table unless you steal money from it.

Albert Einstein

There is a very easy way to return from a casino with a small fortune: go there with a large one.

Jack Yelton

Judged by the dollars spent, gambling is now more popular in America than baseball, the movies and Disneyland combined.

Timothy L. O'Brien, *Bad Bet*

[Gambling] is the child of avarice, the brother of iniquity and the father of mischief.

George Washington

One of the worst things that can happen in life is to win a bet on a horse at an early age.

Danny McGoorty

Lady Godiva put everything she had on a horse.

W. C. Fields

The chance of winning the lottery jackpot is less than that of being struck by lightning. I have never bought a ticket and plan to buy an insulating rubber helmet with the money I save. It will increase my life expectancy by precisely one fourteen-millionth.

Steve Jones

If I had the money and the drinking capacity, I'd probably live at a roulette table and let my life go to hell.

Michael Ventura

He was ... a degenerate gambler. That is, a man who gambled simply to gamble and must lose. As a hero who goes to war must die. Show me a gambler and I'll show you a loser, show me a hero and I'll show you a corpse.

Mario Puzo, referring to Jordan Hawley

There are two times in a man's life when he should not speculate: when he can't afford it, and when he can.

Mark Twain

The safest way to double your money is to fold it over once and put it in your pocket.

Frank McKinney Hubbard

I knew I'd still lost millions of pounds, but I didn't know exactly how many. I was too frightened to find out ... They were just numbers on a screen, nothing to do with real cash.

Nick Leeson

Suckers have no business with money anyway.

Canada Bill Jones, Three Card Monte dealer

A real gentleman, even if he loses everything he owns, must show no emotion. Money must be so far beneath a gentleman that it is hardly worth troubling about.

Fyodor Dostoevsky, *The Gambler*

Horse sense is the thing a horse has which keeps it from betting on people.

W. C. Fields

God

God gave me my money. I believe the power to make money is a gift from God ... it is my duty to make money and still more money and to use the money I make for the good of my fellow man according to the dictates of my conscience.

John D. Rockefeller

If God only gave me a clear sign: like making a large deposit in my name at a Swiss bank.

Woody Allen

Tell God the truth, but give the judge money.

Russian proverb

Religion is what keeps the poor from murdering the rich.

Napoleon Bonaparte

God often pays debts without money.

Irish proverb

When it is a question of money, everyone is of the same religion.

Voltaire

I am a millionaire. That is my religion.

George Bernard Shaw

Money is a wise man's religion.

Euripides, *The Cyclops*

If you want to know what God thinks of money, just look at the people He gave it to.

Dorothy Parker

Commerce has flourished on the skirts of
religion from time immemorial.

John White, *The Golden Cow*

A lot of people are willing to give God the
credit, but not too many are willing to give him
the cash.

Anon

Two things are necessary for the spread of the
Kingdom of God, money and a contempt for
money.

St Augustine

God heals and the doctor takes the fees.

Benjamin Franklin

The meek shall inherit the earth but not the
mineral rights.

John Paul Getty

The Gandhian idea of piety and a very holy poverty is used now to excuse the dirt of the cities, the shoddiness of the architecture. By some inversion, Indians have used the very idea of Gandhi to turn dirt and backwardness into much-loved deities.

V. S. Naipaul

He who serves God for money will serve the devil for better wages.

Sir Roger L'Estrange

Gold

Gold lends a touch of beauty even to the ugly.

Nicolas Boileau

Gold is the sovereign of sovereigns.

Antoine de Rivarol

The barbarous gold barons – they did not find
the gold, they did not mine the gold, they did
not mill the gold, but by some weird alchemy all
the gold belonged to them!

Big Bill Hayward, 1901

There can be no other criterion, no other
standard than gold. Yes, gold which never
changes, which can be shaped into ingots, bars,
coins, which has no nationality and which is
eternally and universally accepted as the
unalterable fiduciary value par excellence.

Charles de Gaulle

Gold-hoarding goes against the American grain;
it fits in better with European pessimism than
with America's traditional optimism.

Paula Nelson

It is much better to have your gold in the hand
than in the heart.

Thomas Fuller

This idol [gold] can boast of two peculiarities;
it is worshipped in all climates, without a single
temple, and by all classes, without a single
hypocrite.

Charles Caleb Colton

Greed

Out upon merry Christmas! What's Christmas time to you but a time for paying bills without money; a time for finding yourself a year older, but not an hour richer.

Ebenezer Scrooge, *A Christmas Carol*

A man is usually more careful of his money than he is of his principles.

Ralph Waldo Emerson

The greed of gain has no time or limit to its capaciousness ... It is ruthlessly ready without a moment's hesitation to crush beauty and life.

Rabindranath Tagore

Those whose life is long still strive for gain, and for all mortals all things take second place to money.

Sophocles

Money changes people just as often as it changes hands.

Al Batt

We are all born brave, trusting and greedy, and most of us remain greedy.

Mignon McLaughlin

The love of money is the root of all evil.

St Paul, 1 Timothy 6:10

Money is the root of all evil, but the foliage is fascinating.

Val Peters

I did not have three thousand pairs of shoes, I had one thousand and sixty.

Imelda Marcos

Money is not the most important thing in the world. Love is. Fortunately, I love money.

Jackie Mason

A man that hoards up riches and enjoys them not is like an ass that carries gold and eats thistles.

Sir Richard Burton

If you would abolish avarice, you must abolish its mother, luxury.

Marcus Tullius Cicero

There are many things that we would throw away, if we were not afraid that others might pick them up.

Oscar Wilde

One of the weaknesses of our age is our apparent inability to distinguish our needs from our greeds.

Don Robinson

One of the evils of money is that it tempts us to look at it rather than at the things that it buys.

E. M. Forster

Greed is all right ... Greed is healthy. You can be greedy and still feel good about yourself.

Ivan F. Boesky

It is partly to avoid consciousness of greed that we prefer to associate with those who are at least as greedy as we ourselves. Those who consume much less are a reproach.

Charles Horton Cooley

When a fellow says, 'It ain't the money but the principle of the thing,' it's the money.

Frank McKinney Hubbard

The discovery of America was the occasion of
the greatest outburst of cruelty and reckless
greed known in history.

Joseph Conrad

If all the rich people in the world divided up
their money amongst themselves there wouldn't
be enough to go around.

Christina Stead

The almighty dollar, that great object of
universal devotion.

Washington Irving

Where large sums of money are concerned, it is
advisable to trust nobody.

Agatha Christie

America is an enormous frosted cupcake in the
middle of millions of starving people.

Gloria Steinem

Poverty wants some things, luxury many, avarice all things.

Abraham Cowley

It is physically impossible for a well-educated, intellectual, or brave man to make money the chief object of his thoughts.

John Ruskin

A moderate addiction to money may not always be hurtful; but when taken in excess it is nearly always bad for the health.

Clarence Day

A wise man should have money in his head, but not in his heart.

Jonathan Swift

Few men have virtue to withstand the highest bidder.

George Washington

People will swim through shit if you put a few bob in it.

> Peter Sellers

Hollywood is a place where they'll pay you a thousand dollars for a kiss and fifty cents for your soul.

> Marilyn Monroe

The point is that you can't be too greedy.

> Donald Trump

One can never be too thin or too rich.

> Wallis Simpson

Happiness

I'm so happy to be rich, I'm willing to take all the consequences.

Howard Abrahamson

Wealth and want equally harden the human heart, like frost and fire both are alien to human flesh.

Theodore Parker

It's possible to own too much. A man with one watch knows what time it is; a man with two watches is never quite sure.

Lee Segall

Wealth is the ability to fully experience life.

Henry David Thoreau

Poor people have more fun than rich people, they say. But I notice it's the rich people who keep saying it.

Jack Paar

What troubles the poor is the money they can't get, and what troubles the rich is the money they can't keep.

Laurence J. Peter

You are going to let the fear of poverty govern your life and your reward will be that you will eat, but you will not live.

George Bernard Shaw

Money is the root of all evil, but it is also the root of all fun.

Mike Culbertson

Wealth is well known to be a great comforter.

Plato

There are people who have money and people who are rich.

Coco Chanel

Fortune and humour govern the world.

François Duc de la Rochefoucauld

Give me the luxuries of life and I will willingly do without the necessities.

Frank Lloyd Wright

It is a wise man that does know the contented man is never poor, whilst the discontented man is never rich.

Frank Herbert

Money won't buy happiness, but it will pay the salaries of a large research staff to study the problem.

Bill Vaughan

While money can't buy happiness, it helps enable you to look for it in comfort.

Anon

A penny will hide the biggest star in the universe if you hold it close enough to your eye.

Samuel Grafton

I asked for riches, that I may be happy; I was given poverty, that I might be wise.

Anon

When I was young, I used to think that wealth and power would bring me happiness ... I was right.

Gahan Wilson

If you teach a poor young man to shave himself, and keep his razor in order, you may contribute more to the happiness of his life than in giving him a thousand guineas.

Benjamin Franklin

It is the great privilege of poverty to be happy and yet unenvied.

Samuel Johnson

It isn't necessary to be rich and famous to be happy. It's only necessary to be rich.

Alan Alda

It is pretty hard to tell what does bring happiness; poverty and wealth have both failed.

Frank McKinney Hubbard

Don't answer back if you're out to make money, but do if you're out for enjoyment.

Barry Pain

I have no money, no resources, no hopes. I am the happiest man alive.

Henry Miller

What's the use of happiness? It can't buy you money.

Henny Youngman

While I'm fully aware that money can't buy happiness, I wouldn't mind being known as that melancholy guy who drives the red Lamborghini Diablo.

George Olson

All I ask is the chance to prove that money can't make me happy.

Spike Milligan

Money doesn't bring happiness, though it has been known to cause an occasional smile.

Herb True

Money can't buy you happiness, but it can buy you a yacht big enough to pull up right alongside it.

David Lee Roth

Whoever said money can't buy happiness, didn't know where to shop.

Anon

Man's greatest joy is to slay his enemy, plunder his riches, ride his steeds, see the tears of his loved ones and embrace his women.

Genghis Khan

The surest way to ruin a man who doesn't know how to handle money is to give him some.

George Bernard Shaw

No illusion is more crucial than the illusion that great success and huge money buy you immunity from the common ills of mankind, such as cars that won't start.

Larry McMurtry

A feast is made for laughter, and wine maketh merry: but money answereth all things.

Ecclesiastes 10:19

Money can't buy happiness the way poverty delivers misery.

Anon

No, not rich. I am a poor man with money, which is not the same thing.

Gabriel García Márquez

Superfluous wealth can buy superfluities only.

Henry David Thoreau

We firmly believe there is more to life than money, beer and sex. We just don't know what it is.

Aaron Shapiro

People say that money is not the key to
happiness, but I always figured if you have
enough money, you can have a key made.

Joan Rivers

We are stripped bare by the curse of plenty.

Winston Churchill

Money is human happiness in the abstract: he,
then, who is no longer capable of enjoying
human happiness in the concrete devotes his
heart entirely to money.

Arthur Schopenhauer

There is nothing more demoralising than a
small but adequate income.

Edmund Wilson

Whenever it is in any way possible, every boy
and girl should choose as his life work some
occupation which he should like to do anyhow,
even if he did not need the money.

William Lyon Phelps

'Poor but happy' is not a phrase invented by a poor person.

Mason Cooley

It is a kind of spiritual snobbery that makes people think that they can be happy without money.

Albert Camus

No matter how hard you hug your money, it never hugs back.

H. Jackson Brown

Bachelors should be heavily taxed. It is not fair that some men should be happier than others.

Oscar Wilde

It is better to work in your own land than to count your money abroad.

Croatian proverb

Our incomes are like our shoes; if too small,
they gall and pinch us; but if too large, they
cause us to stumble and trip.

Charles Caleb Colton

Money gives me more energy than all the
Granola bars in the world.

Mason Cooley

Having money is just the best thing in the world.

Madonna

What's money? A man is a success if he gets up
in the morning and goes to bed at night and in
between does what he wants to do.

Bob Dylan

Worldly riches are like nuts; many clothes
are torn getting them, many a tooth broke in
cracking them, but never a belly filled with
eating them.

Ralph Venning

You can be young without money but you can't be old without it.

Tennessee Williams

I'd like to live like a poor man with lots of money.

Pablo Picasso

Money can't buy friends, but it can get you a better class of enemy.

Spike Milligan

A large income is the best recipe for happiness I ever heard of.

Jane Austen

Annual income twenty pounds, annual expenditure nineteen six, result happiness. Annual income twenty pounds, annual expenditure twenty pounds nought and six, result misery.

Charles Dickens, *David Copperfield*

We do not live to eat and make money. We eat and make money to be able to enjoy life. That is what life means and what life is for.

George Leigh Mallory

Most of the rich people I've known have been fairly miserable.

Agatha Christie

This planet has – or rather had – a problem, which was this: most of the people living on it were unhappy for pretty much of the time. Many solutions were suggested for this problem, but most of these were largely concerned with the movements of small green pieces of paper, which is odd because on the whole it wasn't the small green pieces of paper that were unhappy.

Douglas Adams

Money doesn't make you happy. I now have $50 million but I was just as happy when I had $48 million.

Arnold Schwarzenegger

Liking money like I like it, is nothing less than mysticism. Money is a glory.

Salvador Dalí

Prosperity is living easily and happily in the real world, whether you have money or not.

Jerry Gellis

The seven deadly sins ... Food, clothing, firing, rent, taxes, respectability and children. Nothing can lift those seven millstones from Man's neck but money; and the spirit cannot soar until the millstones are lifted.

George Bernard Shaw

Nothing lulls and inebriates like money; when you have a lot, the world seems a better place than it actually is.

Anton Pavlovich

Have Nots

The argument that the West was somehow to blame for world poverty was itself a Western invention. Like decolonisation, it was a product of guilt, the prime dissolvent of order and justice.

Paul Johnson

What is the matter with the poor is poverty; what is the matter with the rich is uselessness.

George Bernard Shaw

He that wants money, means, and content is without three good friends.

William Shakespeare, *As You Like It*

Come away; poverty's catching.

Aphra Behn, *The Rover*

The discovery of poverty at the beginning of the 1960s was something like the discovery of America almost five hundred years earlier. In the case of these exotic terrains, plenty of people were on the site before the discoverers ever arrived.

Barbara Ehrenreich

In going to America one learns that poverty is not a necessary accompaniment to civilisation.

Oscar Wilde

The richest heritage a young man can have is to be born into poverty.

Andrew Carnegie

One of the strange things about life is that the poor, who need money the most, are the very ones that never have it.

Finley Peter Dunne

I worked my way up from nothing to a state of extreme poverty.

Groucho Marx, *Monkey Business*

Clothes make the poor invisible ... America has the best-dressed poverty the world has ever known.

Michael Harrington

The honest poor can sometimes forget poverty. The honest rich can never forget it.

G. K. Chesterton

As society advances the standard of poverty rises.

Theodore Parker

The right time to dine is: for the rich man, when he is hungry; and for the poor, when he has something to eat.

Mexican proverb

I just need enough to tide me over until I need more.

Bill Hoest

I wasn't born in a log cabin, but my family moved into one as soon as they could afford it.

Melville D. Landon

I want there to be no peasant in my kingdom so poor that he cannot have a chicken in his pot every Sunday.

Henry IV of Navarre

People who are much too sensitive to demand of cripples that they run races ask of the poor that they get up and act just like everybody else in society.

Michael Harrington

To trust people is a luxury in which only the wealthy can indulge; the poor cannot afford it.

E. M. Forster, *Howards End*

The greatest man in history was the poorest.

Emerson

Poverty, to be picturesque, should be rural.
Suburban misery is as hideous as it is pitiable.

Anthony Trollope

Poverty is like punishment for a crime you
didn't commit. And one never really forgets
either – everything serves as a constant reminder
of it.

Eli Khamarov

Moderate poverty can be a blessing.

S. Tsow

When I was a kid in Houston, we were so poor
we couldn't afford the last two letters, so we
called ourselves po'.

George Foreman

There were times my pants were so thin I could sit on a dime and tell if it was heads or tails.

Spencer Tracy

A penny is a lot of money – if you haven't got a penny.

Yiddish proverb

I am having an out-of-money experience.

Anon

Virtues can be afforded only by the poor, who have nothing to lose.

Alexander Chase

What a devil art thou, Poverty! How many desires – how many aspirations after goodness and truth – how many noble thoughts, loving wishes toward our fellows, beautiful imaginings thou hast crushed under thy heel, without remorse or pause!

Walt Whitman

The purpose of a liberal education is to make you philosophical enough to accept the fact that you will never make much money.

Anon

I've never been poor, only broke. Being poor is a frame of mind. Being broke is only a temporary situation.

Mike Todd

The trouble with being poor is that it takes up all your time.

Willem de Kooning

I used to think I was poor. Then they told me I wasn't poor, I was needy. They told me it was self-defeating to think of myself as needy, I was deprived. Then they told me underprivileged was overused. I was disadvantaged. I still don't have a dime. But I have a great vocabulary.

Jules Feiffer

When you ain't got no money, you gotta get an attitude.

Richard Pryor

I'm scared to death of being poor. It's like a fat girl who loses five hundred pounds but is always fat inside. I grew up poor and will always feel poor inside. It's my pet paranoia.

Cher

An individual American could make more money than 93 percent of the other people on the planet and still be considered poor.

P. J. O'Rourke

Society can transport money from the rich to the poor only in a leaky bucket.

Arthur M. Okun

As for the virtuous poor, one can pity them, of course, but one cannot possibly admire them. They have made private terms with the enemy, and sold their birthright for very bad pottage. They must also be extraordinarily stupid.

Oscar Wilde

It would be nice if the poor were to get even half of the money that is spent in studying them.

Bill Vaughan

If you have no money, be polite.

Danish proverb

Poverty is the worst form of violence.

Mahatma Gandhi

Many men of course became extremely rich, but this was perfectly natural and nothing to be ashamed of because no one was really poor, at least no one worth speaking of.

Douglas Adams

It's not hard to tell we was poor – when you saw the toilet paper dryin' on the clothesline.

George Lindsey

Wealth is not without its advantages, and the case to the contrary, although it has often been made, has never proved widely persuasive.

John Kenneth Galbraith

For every talent that poverty has stimulated it has blighted a hundred.

John W. Gardner

I never saw a beggar yet who would recognise guilt if it bit him on his unwashed ass.

Tony Parsons

Now and then you meet a man with such a cordial handclasp and such a friendly personality, you know he hasn't any money.

Anon

We are not concerned with the very poor. They are unthinkable, and only to be approached by the statistician or the poet.

E. M. Forster

Youth is the best time to be rich; and the best time to be poor.

Euripides

Anger makes dull men witty, but it keeps them poor.

Francis Bacon

Give me the poverty that enjoys true wealth.

Henry David Thoreau

Poverty is taking your children to the hospital and spending the whole day waiting with no one even taking your name – and then coming back the next day, and the next, until they finally get around to you.

Janice Bradshaw

Poverty is an anomaly to rich people; it is very difficult to make out why people who want dinner do not ring the bell.

Walter Bagehot

Fivescore years ago, a great American, in whose symbolic shadow we stand today, signed the Emancipation Proclamation ... 100 years later, the Negro lives on a lonely island of poverty in the midst of a vast ocean of material prosperity.

Martin Luther King, Jr, 'I Have A Dream' speech

When I was young, poverty was so common that we didn't know it had a name.

Lyndon B. Johnson

I started out with nothing. I still have most of it.

Michael Davis

Poor people make a very poor business of it when they try to seem rich.

Herman Melville

The two big advantages I had at birth were to have been born wise and to have been born in poverty.

Sophia Loren

He was so broke he couldn't even pay attention.

American saying

Poverty is the parent of revolution and crime.

Aristotle

The modern poor are not pitied ... but written off as trash. The twentieth-century consumer economy has produced the first culture for which a beggar is a reminder of nothing.

John Berger

The leaders of the French Revolution excited the poor against the rich; this made the rich poor, but it never made the poor rich.

Fisher Ames

Necessity never made a good bargain.

Benjamin Franklin

Poverty ... It is life near the bone, where it is sweetest.

Henry David Thoreau

Laziness travels so slowly that poverty soon overtakes him.

Benjamin Franklin

When you don't have any money, the problem is food. When you have money, it's sex. When you have both, it's health.

J. P. Donleavy

Poverty is uncomfortable; but nine times out of ten the best thing that can happen to a young man is to be tossed overboard and compelled to sink or swim.

James A. Garfield

Modern poverty is not the poverty that was blest in the Sermon on the Mount.

George Bernard Shaw

We haven't the money, so we've got to think.

Ernest Rutherford, British physicist

If rich, it is easy enough to conceal our wealth, but, if poor, it is not quite so easy to conceal our poverty. We shall find it is less difficult to hide a thousand guineas, than one hole in our coat.

Charles Caleb Colton

When shit becomes valuable, the poor will be born without assholes.

Henry Miller

I've always been after the trappings of great luxury. But all I've got hold of are the trappings of great poverty. I've got hold of the wrong load of trappings, and a rotten load they are too, ones I could have very well done without.

Peter Cook

131

Poverty must have many satisfactions, else there would not be so many poor people.

Don Herold

Those who have some means think that the most important thing in the world is love. The poor know that it is money.

Gerald Brenan, *Thoughts in a Dry Season*

Errors look so very ugly in persons of small means – one feels they are taking quite a liberty in going astray; whereas people of fortune may naturally indulge in a few delinquencies.

George Eliot, *Janet's Repentance*

The poverty from which I have suffered could be diagnosed as 'Soho' poverty. It comes from having the airs and graces of a genius and no talent.

Quentin Crisp

For one man that can stand prosperity, there are a hundred that will stand adversity.

Thomas Carlyle

The working classes are never embarrassed by money – only the absence of it.

Ken Livingstone

Haves

Don't hate me because I'm beautiful. Hate me because I'm beautiful, smart and rich.

Calvin Keegan

People are fascinated by the rich; Shakespeare wrote plays about kings not beggars.

Dominick Dunne

I have always said that if I were a rich man I would employ a professional praiser.

Osbert Sitwell

I don't wake up for less than $10,000 a day.

Linda Evangelista

Keep company with the very rich and you'll end up picking up the cheque.

Stanley Walker

Money is a wonderful commodity to have, but the more one possesses, the more involved and complicated become his dealings and relationships with people.

John Paul Getty

An advantage of being rich is that all your faults are called eccentricities.

Anon

Everyone's fortune is pure chance and luck, save our own.

Eli Khamarov

You can't have everything. Where would you put it?

Steve Wright

When I have nothing to do at night and can't think, I always iron my money.

Robert Mitchum, *His Kind of Woman*

I don't know much about being a millionaire, but I'll bet I'd be darling at it.

Dorothy Parker

I'd give $1,000 to be a millionaire.

Lewis Timberlake

Affluenza: a psychiatric disturbance arising from an excess of money.

Gary Dunford

What a dignity it gives an old lady, that balance at the bankers! How tenderly we look at her faults if she is a relative; what a kind good-natured old creature we find her!

William Makepeace Thackeray

When I was young I thought that money was the most important thing in life; now that I am old I know that it is.

Oscar Wilde

That's the trouble with being me. At this point, nobody gives a damn what my problem is. I could literally have a tumour on the side of my head and they'd be like, 'Yeah, big deal. I'd eat a tumour every morning for the kinda money you're pulling down.'

Jim Carrey

Shitting is one thing the rich have to do for themselves.

Lindsey Davis

I get so tired listening to one million dollars
here, one million dollars there, it's so petty.

Imelda Marcos

The principal benefit acting has afforded me is
the money to pay for my psychoanalysis.

Marlon Brando

I never heard of an old man forgetting where he
had buried his money! Old people remember
what interests them: the dates fixed for their
lawsuits, and the names of their debtors and
creditors.

Marcus Tullius Cicero

Nothing is more admirable than the fortitude
with which millionaires tolerate the
disadvantages of their wealth.

Rex Stout

138

I must say that I do wrestle with the amount of money I make, but at the end of the day what am I gonna say? I took less money so Rupert Murdoch could have more?

Tom Hanks

It doesn't matter whether you are rich or poor — as long as you've got money.

Joe E. Lewis

But Satan now is wiser than of yore,
And tempts by making rich, not making poor.

Alexander Pope, Epistle to Lord Bathurst

One of the penalties of wealth is that the older you grow, the more people there are in the world who would rather have you dead than alive.

C. H. B. Kitchin

Respectable means rich, and decent means poor. I should die if I heard my family called decent.

Thomas Love Peacock

Every day I get up and look through the Forbes
list of the richest people in America. If I'm not
there, I go to work.

Robert Orben

Money is better than poverty, if only for
financial reasons.

Woody Allen

The prosperous man is never sure that he is
loved for himself.

Lucan

No one would have remembered the Good
Samaritan if he'd only had good intentions. He
had money as well.

Margaret Thatcher

The only way to survive in today's business
world is to have an MBA – a Massive Bank
Account.

Anon

I'd like to have money. And I'd like to be a good writer. These two can come together, and I hope they will, but if that's too adorable, I'd rather have money.

Dorothy Parker

I don't mind their having a lot of money, and I
  don't care how they employ it,
But I do think that they damn well ought to
  admit they enjoy it.

Ogden Nash, 'The Terrible People'

Short of genius, a rich man cannot imagine poverty.

Charles Peguy

Money doesn't change men, it merely unmasks them. If a man is naturally selfish or arrogant or greedy, the money brings that out, that's all.

Henry Ford

I don't know how much money I've got ... I did ask the accountant how much it came to. I wrote it down on a bit of paper. But I've lost the bit of paper.

John Lennon

I never been in no situation where having money make it any worse.

Clinton Jones

In a rich man's house there is no place to spit but his face.

Diogenes of Sinope

The rich are the scum of the earth in every country.

G. K. Chesterton

His money is twice tainted: taint yours and taint mine.

Mark Twain

If you can count your money, you don't have a
billion dollars.

John Paul Getty

The more I see of the moneyed classes, the more
I understand the guillotine.

George Bernard Shaw

Some people's money is merited
And other people's is inherited.

Ogden Nash

Money's a horrid thing to follow, but a
charming thing to meet.

Henry James

I'm not a paranoid deranged millionaire.
Goddamit, I'm a billionaire.

Howard Hughes

Your wealth is good. So why isn't everyone else's wealth good?

P. J. O'Rourke

It is the wretchedness of being rich that you have to live with rich people.

Logan Pearsall Smith

Hope

Americans are optimists. They hope they'll be wealthy someday – and they're positive they can get one more brushful of paint out of an empty can.

Bern Williams

Something will turn up!

Mr MacCawber, *David Copperfield*

He that lives upon hope will die fasting.

Benjamin Franklin

You don't seem to realise that a poor person who is unhappy is in a better position than a rich person who is unhappy. Because the poor person has hope. He thinks money would help.

Jean Kerr

Inflation

Having a little inflation is like being a little pregnant.

Leon Henderson, US economist

Inflation steals from those who still believe in thrift, and robs pensions and retirement funds.

Ron Paul

The cost of living has gone up another dollar a quart.

W. C. Fields

Inflation is the one form of taxation that can be imposed without legislation.

Milton Friedman

Believing in the control of inflation by curbing the money supply! That is like deciding to stop your dog fouling the sidewalk by plugging up its rear end. It is highly unlikely to succeed, but if it does it kills the hound.

Michael D. Stephens

Inflation is bringing us true democracy. For the first time in history, luxuries and necessities are selling at the same price.

Robert Orben

Inflation in the Sixties was a nuisance to be endured, like varicose veins or French foreign policy.

Bernard Levin

Once the printing presses roll, and the decimal points drift to the right, you're done for. It only takes a moment to wipe out a lifetime of careful savings.

James U. Blanchard III

A nickel ain't worth a dime anymore.

Yogi Berra

Inflation is as violent as a mugger, as frightening as an armed robber and as deadly as a hit man.

Ronald Reagan

Inflation allows you to live in a more expensive neighbourhood without moving.

Anon

My dog is worried about the economy because Alpo is up to 99 cents a can. That's almost seven dollars in dog money.

Joe Weinstein

It's a recession when your neighbour loses his job; it's a depression when you lose yours.

Harry S. Truman

Inflation is when you pay fifteen dollars for the ten-dollar haircut you used to get for five dollars when you had hair.

Sam Ewing

One man's wage rise is another man's price increase.

Harold Wilson

A study of economics usually reveals that the best time to buy anything is last year.

Marty Allen

Today you can go to a gas station and find the cash register open and the toilets locked. They must think toilet paper is worth more than money.

Joey Bishop

Investing

Money is like an arm or leg – use it or lose it.

Henry Ford

It is still possible to make a small fortune on dot.coms so long as you start with a large one.

Anon

Nothing is more disastrous than a rational investment in an irrational world.

John Maynard Keynes

If you don't know who you are, the stock market is an expensive place to find out.

Adam Smith

Everyone has the brain power to make money in stocks. Not everyone has the stomach.

Peter Lynch

The main purpose of the stock market is to make fools of as many men as possible.

Bernard M. Baruch

I never attempt to make money on the stock market. I buy on the assumption that they could close the market the next day and not reopen it for five years.

Warren Buffet

Never invest your money in anything that eats or needs repainting.

Billy Rose

We go to the movies to be entertained, not to
see rape, ransacking, pillage and looting. We can
get all that in the stock market.

Kennedy Gammage

I started up an underground paper. I started up
a punk band. I had an upstart TV company …
F**k the Net – I'm already rich!

Bob Geldof

If you can take $20,000 in one-hundred dollar
bills and walk up on a windy hill and tear them
up and watch them blow away, and it doesn't
bother you, then you should go into the
commodities market.

Don Tyson

Internet investors have the brains of grapefruit.
If you started a company called Set Fire to Piles
of Money.com, they'd be beating down your
door.

Dave Barry

Why is the man or woman who invests all your money called a broker?

George Carlin

A speculator is a man who observes the future, and acts before it occurs.

Bernard M. Baruch

You shouldn't own common stocks if a decrease in their value by fifty percent would cause you to feel stress.

Warren Buffet

Put not your trust in money, but put your money in trust.

Oliver Wendell Holmes

$100 placed at seven percent interest compounded quarterly for 200 years will increase to more than $100,000,000 – by which time it will be worth nothing.

Robert A. Heinlein

If a man empties his purse into his head, no man can take it away from him. An investment in knowledge always pays the best interest.

Benjamin Franklin

I buy when other people are selling.

John Paul Getty

Anyone who thinks there's safety in numbers hasn't looked at the stock market pages.

Irene Peter

If investing is entertaining, if you're having fun, you're probably not making any money. Good investing is boring.

George Soros

A stockbroker is someone who takes your money and invests it until it's all gone.

Woody Allen

Love

Bart! With $10,000, we'd be millionaires! We could buy all kinds of useful things like ... love!

Homer Simpson

I'd asked around ten or fifteen people for suggestions ... Finally one lady friend asked the right question, 'Well, what do you love most?' That's how I started painting money.

Andy Warhol

Money is a singular thing. It ranks with love as man's greatest source of joy. And with death as his greatest source of anxiety.

John Kenneth Galbraith

Money, it seems, attracts more envy than empathy. More lust than love.

Cary Grant

Money cannot buy the fuel of love but is excellent kindling.

W. H. Auden

Money can buy the most expensive dog in the world, but only love can make him wag his tail.

Anon

It isn't enough for you to love money – it's also necessary that money should love you.

Baron Rothschild

Money can't buy love, but it improves your bargaining position.

Christopher Marlowe

Of all the icy blasts that blow on love, a request
for money is the most chilling and havoc
wreaking.

Gustave Flaubert

I have imbibed such a love for money that I
keep some sequins in a drawer to count, and cry
over them once a week.

Lord Byron

Money is like love; it kills slowly and painfully
the one who withholds it, and enlivens the other
who turns it on his fellow man.

Kahlil Gibran

Making It

When a problem presents itself, beware not to accept it at face value ... A problem to others may be the means for you to become extremely wealthy.

Kurt Hanks

Don't stay in bed, unless you can make money in bed.

George Burns

Sudden success in golf is like the sudden acquisition of wealth. It is apt to unsettle and deteriorate the character.

P. G. Wodehouse

Wealth is not a matter of intelligence, it's a matter of inspiration.

Jim Rohn

There is no money to be made at the bottom. There's no money to be made in the middle. But there's a lot to be made at the top.

Martin Zimet

Formal education will make you a living; self-education will make you a fortune.

Jim Rohn

If you really need money, you can sell your kidney or even your car.

Homer Simpson

If we could sell our experiences for what they cost us we'd be millionaires.

Abigail Van Baren

There's no embarrassing way to earn money.

Richard Fish, *Ally McBeal*

Money is like promises – easier made than kept.

Josh Billings

Paying attention to simple little things that most men ignore makes a few men rich.

Henry Ford

Sell your soul to yourself. You'll make more money.

Marilyn Manson

If you wonder why something is the way it is, find out who's making money from it being that way.

Anon

Right now I'd do anything for money. I'd kill
somebody for money. I'd kill you for money.
Ha ha ha. Ah, no. You're my friend. I'd kill you
for nothing.

Chico Marx, *The Coconuts*

My formula for success is rise early, work late,
and strike oil.

John Paul Getty

Don't be too busy earning a living to make any
money.

Joe Karbo

Beauty is only skin deep, but it's a valuable asset
if you're poor or haven't any sense.

Frank McKinney Hubbard

The advantage of a classical education is that
it enables you to despise the wealth that it
prevents you from achieving.

Russell Green

Pennies don't fall from heaven. They have to be earned on earth.

Margaret Thatcher

Make money and the whole nation will conspire to call you a gentleman.

George Bernard Shaw

I do everything for a reason, most of the time the reason is money.

Suzy Parker

However toplofty and idealistic a man may be, he can always rationalise his right to earn money.

Raymond Chandler

The trouble you can get into, just 'cause you want five thousand bucks.

Daffy Duck

The shortest and best way to make your fortune
is to let people see clearly that it is in their
interests to promote yours.

Jean de la Bruyère

It requires a great deal of boldness and a great
deal of caution to make a great fortune, and
when you have it, it requires ten times as much
skill to keep it.

Ralph Waldo Emerson

Always remember, money isn't everything – but
also remember to make a lot of it before talking
such fool nonsense.

Earl Wilson

It's easy to sit there and say you'd like to have
more money. And I guess that's what I like
about it. It's easy. Just sitting there, rocking back
and forth, wanting that money.

Jack Handey

I plan to have character one day, great character, but if you want to be rich you better get the money before the scruples set in.

Richard Fish, *Ally McBeal*

The more money an American accumulates, the less interesting he becomes.

Gore Vidal

It isn't as important to buy as cheap as possible as it is to buy at the right time.

Jesse Livermore

Never knew how poor I was until I started making money.

Gekko, *Wall Street*

Americans make money by playing 'money games', namely mergers, acquisitions, by simply moving money back and forth ... instead of creating and producing goods with some actual value.

Akio Morita, chairman of Sony

Lack of money is no obstacle. Lack of an idea is an obstacle.

Ken Hakuta

The way to wealth is as plain as the way to market. It depends chiefly on two words, industry and frugality; that is waste neither time nor money, but make the best of both.

Benjamin Franklin

I have ways of making money that you know nothing of.

John D. Rockefeller

Money will come when you are doing the right thing.

Mike Phillips

Money never starts an idea. It is always the idea that starts the money.

Owen Laughlin

You can make a lot of money in this game. Just ask my ex-wives. Both of them are so rich that neither of their husbands work.

Lee Trevino

As one digs deeper into the national character of the Americans, one sees that they have sought the value of everything in this world only in the answer to this single question: how much money will it bring in?

Alexis de Tocqueville

Information is money, but data is squat.

Angela Llama-Butler

No one in this world, so far as I know ... has ever lost money by underestimating the intelligence of the great masses of the plain people.

H. L. Mencken

I sell, therefore I am. You buy, therefore I eat.

Craig Dormanen

What better way to prove that you understand a subject than to make money out of it?

Harold Rosenberg

I don't mind that I'm fat. You still get the same money.

Marlon Brando

If small money does not go out, big money will not come in.

Chinese proverb

Rockefeller made his money in oil, which he discovered at the bottom of wells. Oil was considered crude in those days, but so was Rockefeller. Now both are considered quite refined.

Richard Armour

The only reason I'm in Hollywood is that I don't have the moral courage to refuse the money.

Marlon Brando

Prosperity belongs to those who learn new things the fastest.

Paul Zane Pilzer

Most men love money and security more, and creation and construction less, as they get older.

John Maynard Keynes

There are two things needed in these days: first, for rich men to find out how poor men live; and second, for poor men to know how rich men work.

Edward Atkinson

There's no such thing as a free lunch.

Milton Friedman

To kill a relative of whom you are tired is one thing. But to inherit his property afterwards, that is a genuine pleasure.

Honoré de Balzac

The darkest hour of any man's life is when he sits down to plan how to get money without earning it.

Horace Greely

He made his money the really old-fashioned way. He inherited it.

A. J. Carothers

Journalism could be described as turning one's enemies into money.

Craig Brown

I had no ambition to make a fortune. Mere money-making has never been my goal, I had an ambition to build.

John D. Rockefeller

Entrepreneurs are simply those who understand that there is little difference between obstacle and opportunity and are able to turn both to their advantage.

Victor Kiam

Early to bed and early to rise – till you get enough money to do otherwise.

Laurence J. Peter

Entrepreneurship is the last refuge of the trouble-making individual.

Mason Cooley

In the days when the nation depended on agriculture for its wealth it made the Lord Chancellor sit on a woolsack to remind him where the wealth came from. I would like to suggest we remove that now and make him sit on a crate of machine tools.

Prince Philip

The entire essence of America is the hope to first make money – then make money with money – then make lots of money with lots of money.

Paul Erdman

Writing is the only profession where no one considers you ridiculous if you earn no money.

Jules Renard

At my lemonade stand I used to give the first glass away free and charge five dollars for the second glass. The refill contained the antidote.

Emo Phillips

Always try to rub up against money, for if you rub up against money long enough, some of it may rub off on you.

Damon Runyon

I was part of that strange race of people aptly described as spending their lives doing things they detest to make money they don't want to buy things they don't need to impress people they dislike.

Emile Henry Gauvreau

Making money is pretty pointless and it needs constant attention.

Adam Faith

Many people seem to think that opportunity means a chance to get money without earning it.

Anon

Hollywood held this double lure for me, tremendous sums of money for work that required no more effort than a game of pinochle.

Ben Hecht

To make a million, start with $900,000.

Morton Shulman

When a man tells you that he got rich through hard work, ask him: 'Whose?'

Don Marquis

You have to decide whether you want to make money or make sense, because the two are mutually exclusive.

Richard Buckminster Fuller

The secret of getting rich is not to work hard, but to get a lot of other people to work hard for you.

Michael Parenti

It is not that pearls fetch a high price because men have dived for them; but on the contrary, men dive for them because they fetch a high price.

Richard Whately

Now You See It . . .

Money ... has become a sort of railway shunting yard which is forever receiving the wishes and dreams of countless people and dispatching them to unimagined destinations.

James Buchan

Fame vaporises, money goes with the wind, and all that's left is character.

O. J. Simpson

It doesn't make any difference how much
money a father earns, his name is always Dad-
Can-I … Like all other children, my five have
one great talent: they are gifted beggars. Not
one of them ever ran into the room, looked up
at me and said, 'I'm really happy that you're my
father, and as a tangible token of my
appreciation here's a dollar.'

Bill Cosby

Lovers' quarrels are not generally about money.
Divorce cases generally are.

Mason Cooley

Money itself isn't lost or made, it's simply
transferred from one perception to another. This
painting here. I bought it ten years ago for sixty
thousand. I could sell it today for six hundred.
The illusion has become real and the more real
it becomes, the more desperately they want it.

Oliver Stone

Growing up is that slow, painful transition from praying that your face will clear to praying that your cheque will clear.

Anon

The shortest recorded period of time lies between the minute you put some money away for a rainy day and the unexpected arrival of rain.

Jane Bryant Quinn

The way money goes so fast these days, they should paint racing stripes on it.

Mark Russell

Time is waste of money.

Oscar Wilde

Hollywood money isn't money. It's congealed snow, melts in your hand, and there you are.

Dorothy Parker

Politics and Politicians

Poor George [Bush], he can't help it. He was born with a silver foot in his mouth.

Ann Richards

The hopes of the Republic cannot forever tolerate either undeserved poverty or self-serving wealth.

Franklin D. Roosevelt

There is no such thing as government money.

Margaret Thatcher

When they asked George Washington for his
ID, he just took out a quarter.

Stephen Wright

Did you ever figure it out? Taxes is all there is to
politics.

Will Rogers

I was alarmed at my doctor's report: he said I
was sound as a dollar.

Ronald Reagan

'Resource-constrained environment' [are] fancy
Pentagon words that mean there isn't enough
money to go around.

General John W. Vessey, Jr

Only government can take perfectly good paper,
cover it with perfectly good ink and make the
combination worthless.

Milton Friedman

If you have been voting for politicians who promise to give you goodies at someone else's expense, then you have no right to complain when they take your money and give it to someone else, including themselves.

Thomas Sowell

Government is the great fiction, through which everybody endeavours to live at the expense of everybody else.

Frédéric Bastiat

We Asians are the original Conservatives because for thousands of years we have believed in free enterprise ... you have just stolen our philosophy.

Jayvantsinnji Gohel

Republicans have been accused of abandoning the poor. It's the other way around. They never vote for us.

Dan Quayle

Politics has become so expensive that it takes a lot of money even to be defeated.

Will Rogers

They have the usual socialist disease; they have run out of other people's money.

Margaret Thatcher

As soon as you bring up money, I notice, conversation gets sociological, then political, then moral.

Kate Smiley

It is a popular delusion that the government wastes vast amounts of money through inefficiency and sloth. Enormous effort and elaborate planning are required to waste this much money.

P. J. O'Rourke

It's a terribly hard job to spend a billion dollars and get your money's worth.

George M. Humphrey, US Secretary of the Treasury

Politics is the art of getting money from the rich and votes from the poor, with the pretext of protecting one from the other.

Anon

I am not prepared to accept the economics of a housewife.

Jacques Chirac referring to Margaret Thatcher, 1987

I have to work. It costs a lot of money to support a Senator.

Bill Clinton

If only Bapu [Gandhi] knew the cost of setting him up in poverty!

Sarojini Naidu

Government does not solve problems; it subsidises them.

Ronald Reagan

If elected President, I will balance the budget in five years.

Bill Clinton, 1992

We must not set any specific date for balancing the budget.

Bill Clinton, 1994

The budget cannot be balanced in seven years without hurting too many people. We should balance it in ten years.

Bill Clinton, 1995

Poverty mostly affects the poor.

Richard Nixon

The first panacea for a mismanaged nation is inflation of the currency; the second is war. Both bring a temporary prosperity; both bring a permanent ruin. But both are the refuge of political and economic opportunists.

Ernest Hemingway

Power

Those who profit are the ones at the top. They keep the doughnut for themselves and give the hole to the people.

Alexander Lebed

People say law but they mean wealth.

Ralph Waldo Emerson

It's hard being black. You ever been black? I was black once – when I was poor.

Larry Holmes

Money is the string with which a sardonic
destiny directs the motions of its puppets.

Somerset Maugham

Money without brains is always dangerous.

Napoleon Hill

Neither great poverty nor great riches will hear
reason.

Henry Fielding

Beauty is potent, but money is omnipotent.

Anon

Where money talks, there are few interruptions.

Herbert V. Prochnow

Laws grind the poor, and rich men rule the law.

Oliver Goldsmith, *The Traveller*

It's the rich you can terrorise. The poor have nothing to lose.

Imelda Marcos

It is more rewarding to watch money change the world than watch it accumulate.

Gloria Steinem

The rich will do anything for the poor but get off their backs.

Karl Marx

Once upon a time my political opponents honoured me as possessing the fabulous intellectual and economic power by which I created a worldwide depression all by myself.

Herbert Hoover

No place is so strongly fortified that money could not capture it.

Marcus Tullius Cicero

We didn't exactly believe your story, Miss
O'Shea, we believed your two hundred dollars.

Sam Spade, *The Maltese Falcon*

Without money honour is merely a disease.

Jean Racine

Just think what Jesus could have achieved if he'd
only had the money.

Michael Bradley

The buck stops with the guy who signs the
cheques.

Rupert Murdoch

The poor have sometimes objected to being
governed badly; the rich have always objected to
being governed at all.

G. K. Chesterton

We paid three billion dollars for these television stations. We'll decide what the news is. News is what we say it is.

David Boylan, Fox Television manager

Money is the most egalitarian force in society. It confers power on whoever holds it.

Roger Starr

Money doesn't mind if we say it's evil, it goes from strength to strength. It's a fiction, an addiction, and a tacit conspiracy.

Martin Amis

The chief value of money lies in the fact that one lives in a world in which it is overestimated.

H. L. Mencken

Virtue has never been as respectable as money.

Mark Twain

Money speaks sense in a language all nations understand.

Aphra Behn, *The Rover*

In every well-governed state, wealth is a sacred thing; in democracies it is the only sacred thing.

Anatole France

Blood's not thicker than money.

Groucho Marx, *Double Dynamite*

When you've got them by their wallets, their hearts and minds will follow.

Fern Naito

In a terrible crisis there is only one element more helpless than the poor, and that is the rich.

Clarence Darrow

There are two fools in this world. One is the millionaire who thinks that by hoarding money he can somehow accumulate real power, and the other is the penniless reformer who thinks that if only he can take the money from one class and give it to another, all the world's ills will be cured.

Henry Ford

The only reason to have money is to tell any SOB in the world to go to hell.

Humphrey Bogart

It's going to be fun to watch and see how long the meek can keep the earth after they inherit it.

Frank McKinney Hubbard

A poor relation is the most irrelevant thing in nature.

Charles Lamb

Saving

Between work and family, I'm really not
spending enough quality time with my money.

Wall Street Journal cartoon caption

Economy, the poor man's mint.

Martin Tupper

Find a penny, pick it up and all day long you'll
have ... a penny.

Clive Holland

A dollar saved is a quarter earned.

John Ciardi

A simple fact that is hard to learn is that the
time to save money is when you have some.

Joe Moore

Old men are always advising young men to save
money. That is bad advice. Don't save every
nickel. Invest in yourself. I never saved a dollar
until I was forty years old.

Henry Ford

Saving is a very fine thing. Especially when your
parents have done it for you.

Sir Winston Churchill

It wasn't raining when Noah built the ark.

Howard Ruff

Simply by not owning three medium-sized
castles in Tuscany I have saved enough money
in the last forty years on insurance premiums
alone to buy a medium-sized castle in Tuscany.

Ludwig Mies van der Rohe

My mother had to send me to the movies with my birth certificate, so that I wouldn't have to pay the extra fifty cents that the adults had to pay.

Kareem Abdul-Jabar, NBA basketball player

Moderation is the last refuge for the unimaginative.

Oscar Wilde

Thrift is too late at the bottom of the purse.

Seneca

I have enough money to last me the rest of my life, unless I buy something.

Jackie Mason

Save a little money each month and at the end of the year you'll be surprised at how little you have.

Ernest Haskins

A short cut to riches is to subtract from our desires.

Francesco Petrarch

Sex and Marriage

Money, it turned out, was exactly like sex: you thought of nothing else if you didn't have it and thought of other things if you did.

James A. Baldwin

Marriage is like a bank account. You put it in, you take it out, you lose interest.

Irwin Corey

Sex and taxes are in many ways the same. Tax does to cash what males do to genes. It dispenses assets among the population as a whole.

Steve Jones

Like dear St Francis of Assisi I am wedded to
poverty: but in my case the marriage is not a
success.

Oscar Wilde

Millionaires are marrying their secretaries
because they are so busy making money they
haven't time to see other girls.

Doris Lilly

There's a way of transferring funds that is even
faster than electronic banking. It's called marriage.

James Holt McGavran

Money is not an aphrodisiac; the desire it may
kindle in the female eye is more for the cash
than the carrier.

Marya Mannes

Paying alimony is like feeding hay to a dead
horse.

Groucho Marx

Single women have a dreadful propensity for being poor – which is one very strong argument in favour of matrimony.

Jane Austen, letter to Fanny Knight

If there's one thing better than marrying a millionaire, it's divorcing him.

Anon

Poverty keeps together more homes than it breaks up.

H. H. Munro

If income tax is the price you have to pay to keep the government on its feet, alimony is the price we have to pay for sweeping a woman off hers.

Groucho Marx

I bet that if you actually read the entire vastness of the US Tax Code, you'd find at least one sex scene.

Dave Barry

If you marry for money, you will surely earn it.

Ezra Bowen

The way taxes are, you might as well marry for love.

Joe E. Lewis

This would be a much better world if more married couples were as deeply in love as they are in debt.

Earl Wilson

People make love for so many crazy reasons – why shouldn't money be one of them?

Ben Gazzara, *Saint Jack*

The poor wish to be rich, the rich wish to be happy, the single wish to be married, and the married wish to be dead.

Ann Landers

I'd marry again if I found a man who had
fifteen million dollars, would sign over half to
me, and guarantee that he'd be dead within a
year.

Bette Davis

Dating means doing a lot of fun things you will
never do again if you get married. The fun stops
with marriage because you're trying to save
money for when you split up your property.

Dave Barry

Spending It

Sir, I have two very cogent reasons for not
printing any list of subscribers; one, that I have
lost all the names, the other, that I have spent
all the money.

Samuel Johnson

Why is there so much month left at the end of
the money?

John Barrymore

Blackadder: Baldrick, how did you manage to find a turnip that cost £400,000?
Baldrick: Well, I had to haggle . . .

I have no one to leave the money to. I'm a single man. I like spending my money.

Sir Elton John

An annuity is a very serious business.

Jane Austen, *Sense and Sensibility*

I think a lot of people who have just got rich go out and spend their money recklessly on things like investments and their kids' education when they could more wisely buy stuff that will always be valuable like very trendy clothes, holidays and haircuts.

Ali G

You can live well if you're rich and you can live well if you're poor, but if you're poor, it's much cheaper.

Andrew Tobias

There are three easy ways of losing money –
racing is the quickest, women the most pleasant
and farming the most certain.

Lord Amherst

Just pretending to be rich keeps some people poor.

Anon

Money creates taste.

Jenny Holzer

Advertising is usually a trick to get you to spend
money by telling you how much you can save.

Anon

A budget is just a method of worrying before
you spend money, as well as afterward.

Anon

The only question with wealth is, what do you
do with it?

John D. Rockefeller

It takes money to look this cheap.

Dolly Parton

Wealth unused might as well not exist.

Aesop

You never realise how short a month is until you pay alimony.

John Barrymore

On packing: lay out all your clothes and all your money. Then, take half the clothes and twice the money.

Susan Butler Anderson

Every man is rich or poor according to the proportion between his desires and his enjoyments.

Samuel Johnson

There was a time when a fool and his money were soon parted, but now it happens to everybody.

Adlai E. Stevenson

Right now it's only a notion, but I think I can get the money to make it into a concept, and later turn it into an idea.

Woody Allen

To understand someone, find out how he spends his money.

Mason Cooley

Beware of little expenses; a small leak will sink a great ship.

Benjamin Franklin

Everything is on such a clear financial basis in France. It is the simplest country to live in. No one makes things complicated by becoming your friend for any obscure reason. If you want people to like you you have only to spend a little money.

Ernest Hemingway

I only want enough to keep body and soul apart.

Dorothy Parker

In spite of the cost of living, it's still popular.

Laurence J. Peter

My problem lies in reconciling my gross habits
with my net income.

Errol Flynn

No man is rich enough to buy back his past.

Oscar Wilde

Do you know New York stifles me? It makes me
so unhappy. There are so many things I want,
and so many things I cannot afford to have. I
don't see how people ever have money enough
to live here.

Dorothy Gish

Eighty percent of the people of Britain want
more money spent on public transport – in order
that other people will travel on the buses so that
there is more room for them to drive their cars.

John Selwyn Gummer

Oh, for the good old days when people would stop Christmas shopping when they ran out of money.

Anon

It's our money, and we're free to spend it any way we please.

Rose Kennedy on her son John F. Kennedy's presidential campaign

It is not a custom with me to keep money to look at.

George Washington

Any man who has $10,000 left when he dies is a failure.

Errol Flynn

Half the money I spend on advertising is wasted; the trouble is I don't know which half.

John Wanamaker

See, when the government spends money, it creates jobs; whereas when the money is left in the hands of taxpayers, God only knows what they do with it. Bake it into pies, probably. Anything to avoid creating jobs.

Dave Barry

It is better to live rich than to die rich.

Samuel Johnson

Money cannot buy health, but I'd settle for a diamond-studded wheelchair.

Dorothy Parker

Money is of no value; it cannot spend itself. All depends on the skill of the spender.

Ralph Waldo Emerson

Money dignifies what is frivolous if unpaid for.

Virginia Woolf

Yes, I like flowers.

Elton John about the £293,000 spent on flowers

Money is only useful when you get rid of it. It is like the odd card in 'Old Maid': the player who is finally left with it has lost.

Evelyn Waugh

Take It
Or Leave It

Of course I despise money when I haven't got any. It's the only dignified thing to do.

Agatha Christie

Actually, I have no regard for money. Aside from its purchasing power, it's completely useless as far as I'm concerned.

Alfred Hitchcock

Those who condemn wealth are those who have none and see no chance of getting it.

William Penn Patrick

Money isn't everything ... but it ranks right up there with oxygen.

Rita Davenport

Money means nothing to me. Do you think I'd treat my parents' house this way if it did?

Steff, *Pretty in Pink*

The only thing I like about rich people is their money.

Lady Nancy Astor

I'm not money hungry ... People who are rich want to be richer, but what's the difference? You can't take it with you. The toys get different, that's all. The rich guys buy a football team, the poor guys buy a football. It's all relative.

Martina Navratilova

I think money is on the way out.

Anita Loos

I have never been a material girl. My father always told me never to love anything that cannot love you back.

Imelda Marcos

Wealth establishes a man as a hero, and so does poverty.

Andrea Dworkin

Riches have never fascinated me, unless combined with the greatest charm or distinction.

F. Scott Fitzgerald

You have reached the pinnacle of success as soon as you become uninterested in money, compliments, or publicity.

Orlando A. Battista

I have enough money to get by. I'm not independently wealthy, just independently lazy, I suppose.

Montgomery Clift

I don't want money. It is only people who pay
their bills who want that, and I never pay mine.

Oscar Wilde

I don't want to make money, I just want to be
wonderful.

Marilyn Monroe

Having money is rather like being a blond. It is
more fun but not vital.

Mary Quant

We all need money, but there are degrees of
desperation.

Anthony Burgess

Taxes

We contend that for a nation to try to tax itself into prosperity is like a man standing in a bucket and trying to lift himself up by the handle.

Winston Churchill

I told the Inland Revenue I didn't owe them a penny because I lived near the seaside.

Ken Dodd

Some accountants are comedians, but comedians are never accountants.

George Carman about Ken Dodd

The government deficit is the difference between the amount of money the government spends and the amount it has the nerve to collect.

Sam Ewing

When it comes to finances, remember that there are no withholding taxes on the wages of sin.

Mae West

The invention of the teenager was a mistake. Once you identify a period of life in which people get to stay out late but don't have to pay taxes – naturally, nobody wants to live any other way.

Judith Martin

In this world, nothing is certain but death and taxes.

Benjamin Franklin

The avoidance of taxes is the only intellectual pursuit that still carries any reward.

John Maynard Keynes

Did you ever think what the word 'vote' means?
To me it means: 'Voice of Taxpayers Everywhere'.

Martin Buxbaum

The government's view of the economy could be
summed up in a few short phrases: if it moves,
tax it. If it keeps moving, regulate it. And if it
stops moving, subsidise it.

Ronald Reagan

I'm proud to be paying taxes in the United
States. The only thing is – I could be just as
proud for half the money.

Arthur Godfrey

The Eiffel Tower is the Empire State Building
after taxes.

Anon

All taxes paid over a lifetime by the average
American are spent by the government in less
than a second.

Jim Fiebig

The rich aren't like us; they pay less taxes.

Peter De Vries

In general, the art of government consists in taking as much money as possible from one party of the citizens to give to the other.

Voltaire

Governments last as long as the undertaxed can defend themselves against the overtaxed.

Bernard Berenson

When you are skinning your customers you should leave some skin on to grow again so that you can skin them again.

Nikita Khrushchev

I don't know if I can live on my income or not – the government won't let me try it.

Bob Thaves

A dog who thinks he is a man's best friend is a dog who obviously has never met a tax lawyer.

Fran Lebowitz

I love to go to Washington – if only to be near my money.

Bob Hope

I never can pass by the Metropolitan Museum of Art in New York without thinking of it not as a gallery of living portraits but as a cemetery of tax-deductible wealth.

Lewis H. Lapham

The income tax people are very nice. They're letting me keep my own mother.

Henny Youngman

I'm not black or white, I'm a taxpayer.

James Brown

Nothing makes a man and wife feel closer these days than a joint tax return.

Gil Stern

The art of government is to make two-thirds of a nation pay all it possibly can pay for the benefit of the other third.

Voltaire

If the Lord had meant us to pay income taxes, he'd have made us smart enough to prepare the return.

Kirk Kirkpatrick

Why, oh why do we pay taxes, huh?! Just so we can have bloody parking restrictions, and bloody ugly traffic wardens, and bollocky pedestrian bloody crossings!! ...Why not just have a 'Stupidity Tax'? Just tax the stupid people!!

Eddie, *Absolutely Fabulous*

The primary requisite for any new tax law is
for it to exempt enough voters to win the next
election.

Anon

All money nowadays seems to be produced with
a natural homing instinct for the Treasury.

Prince Philip

If you make any money, the government shoves
you in the creek once a year with it in your
pockets, and all that don't get wet you can keep.

Will Rogers

There's nothing wrong with the younger
generation that becoming taxpayers won't cure.

Dan Bennett

Next to being shot at and missed, nothing is
really quite as satisfying as an income tax
refund.

F. J. Raymond

There is just one thing I can promise you about the outer-space programme – your tax-dollar will go further.

Werner von Braun

What is the difference between a taxidermist and a tax collector? The taxidermist takes only your skin.

Mark Twain

It's income tax time again, Americans: time to gather up those receipts, get out those tax forms, sharpen up that pencil, and stab yourself in the aorta.

Dave Barry

Last year I had difficulty with my income tax. I tried to take my analyst off as a business deduction. The government said it was entertainment. We compromised finally and made it a religious contribution.

Woody Allen

The nation ought to have a tax system which looks like someone designed it on purpose.

William E. Simon

The art of taxation consists in so plucking the goose as to obtain the largest amount of feathers with the least possible amount of hissing.

J. B. Colbert

Where there's a will, there's an inheritance tax.

Anon

Day in and day out, your tax accountant can make or lose you more money than any single person in your life, with the possible exception of your kids.

Harvey Mackay

The hardest thing in the world to understand is income tax.

Albert Einstein

When everybody has got money they cut taxes, and when they're broke they raise 'em. That's statesmanship of the highest order.

Will Rogers

Wages

The pay is good and I can walk to work.

John F. Kennedy explaining why he liked being President

Most people work just hard enough not to get fired and get paid just enough money not to quit.

George Carlin

If you don't want to work, you have to work to earn enough money so that you won't have to work.

Ogden Nash

The salary of the chief executive of the large corporation is not a market award for achievement. It is frequently in the nature of a warm personal gesture by the individual to himself.

John Kenneth Galbraith

It's called 'take-home pay' because there's nowhere else you can go with it.

Anon

Men who do things without being told draw the most wages.

Edwin H. Stuart

'Cheque enclosed' are the two most beautiful words in the English language.

Dorothy Parker

Give the labourer his wages before his perspiration be dry.

Mohammed

War

One difference between French appeasement
and American appeasement is that France pays
ransom in cash and gets its hostages back while
the United States pays ransom in arms and gets
additional hostages taken.

William L. Safire

I had supposed that most people liked money
better than almost anything else, but I discovered
that they liked destruction even better.

Bertrand Russell

Wars on nations change maps. War on poverty
maps change.

Muhammed Ali

There are evils ... that have the ability to
survive identification and go on for ever ...
money, for instance, or war.

Saul Bellow

When the rich wage war, it's the poor who die.

Jean-Paul Sartre

Wars are caused by undefended wealth.

Douglas MacArthur

I have gone to war too ... I am going to fight
capitalism even if it kills me. It is wrong that
people like you should be comfortable and
well fed while all around you people are
starving.

Sylvia Pankhurst

I predict you will sink step by step into a
bottomless quagmire, however much you spend
in men and money.

General Charles de Gaulle on the Vietnam War

What a country calls its vital economic interests are not the things which enable its citizens to live, but the things which enable it to make war.

Simone Weil

What's It Worth?

Today the greatest single source of wealth is
between your ears.

Brian Tracy

Money can be more of a barrier between people
than language or race or religion.

Vera Caspary

Don't judge men's wealth or godliness by their
Sunday appearance.

Benjamin Franklin

Adversity makes men, and prosperity makes monsters.

Victor Hugo

Money isn't everything, but it's a long way ahead of what comes next.

Edmund Stockdale

Advertising is a valuable economic factor because it is the cheapest way of selling goods, particularly if the goods are worthless.

Sinclair Lewis

We can tell our values by looking at our chequebook stubs.

Gloria Steinem

No man will take counsel, but every man will take money; therefore, money is better than counsel.

Jonathan Swift

A man may be a tough, concentrated, successful money-maker and never contribute to his country anything more than a horrible example.

Robert Menzies

If a man is after money, he's money mad; if he keeps it, he's a capitalist; if he spends it, he's a playboy; if he doesn't get it, he's a never-do-well; if he doesn't try to get it, he lacks ambition; if he gets it without working for it, he's a parasite; and if he accumulates it after a lifetime of hard work, people call him a fool who never got anything out of life.

Vic Oliver

As long as people will accept crap, it will be financially profitable to dispense it.

Dick Cavett

Money is the moment to me. Money is my mood.

Andy Warhol

Education costs money, but then so does ignorance.

Sir Claus Moser

Almost everything on earth can be manufactured a little less well and be sold for a little less money.

John Ruskin

Money is our madness, our vast collective madness.

D. H. Lawrence

Yesterday is a cancelled cheque. Tomorrow is a promissary note. Today is cash.

Anon

There's nothing wrong with cash. It gives you time to think.

Robert Prechter, Jr

Money, like vodka, turns a person into an eccentric.

Anton Chekhov

I make a lot of money, but I don't want to talk about that. I work very hard and I'm worth every cent.

Naomi Campbell

Money is a guarantee that we may have what we want in the future. Though we need nothing at the moment, it insures the possibility of satisfying a necessary desire when it arises.

Aristotle

Money is to my social existence what health is to my body.

Mason Cooley

Wealth, in even the most improbable cases, manages to convey the aspect of intelligence.

John Kenneth Galbraith

Money is a kind of poetry.

Wallace Stevens

Money is the root of all evil, and yet it is such a useful root that we cannot get on without it any more than we can without potatoes.

Louisa May Alcott

Dope will get you through times of no money better than money will get you through times of no dope.

Gilbert Shelton

Money has no moral opinions.

Abraham Polonsky

Comparatively few people know what a million dollars actually is. To the majority it is a gaseous concept, swelling or decreasing as the occasion suggests.

Robertson Davies

Life is a dream for the wise, a game for the fool,
a comedy for the rich, a tragedy for the poor.

Sholom Aleichem

Price is what you pay. Value is what you get.

Warren Buffet

If it's free, it's probably not worth a damn.

Don Stepp

What's a thousand dollars? Mere chicken feed. A
poultry matter.

Groucho Marx

Money, like number and law, is a category of
thought.

Oswald Spengler

Women

Nearly every glamorous, wealthy, successful
career woman you might envy now started out
as some kind of schlepp.

Helen Gurley Brown

Even more than the Pill, what has liberated
women is that they no longer need to depend
on men economically.

Jane Bryant Quinn

Society has never barred women from bread-
winning roles, but only from economic roles
that are profitable and respectable.

Jeane Kirkpatrick

Women prefer men who have something tender about them – especially legal tender.

Kay Ingram

A man is a person that will pay two dollars for a one dollar item he wants. A woman will pay one dollar for a two dollar item she doesn't want.

William Binger

A successful man is one who makes more money than his wife can spend. A successful woman is one who can find such a man.

Lana Turner

You like money. You got a great big dollar sign there where most women have a heart.

Stanley Kubrick

If American men are obsessed with money, American women are obsessed with weight. The men talk of gain, the women talk of loss, and I do not know which talk is the more boring.

Marya Mannes

A fool and her money are soon courted.

Helen Rowland

Women want men, careers, money, children, friends, luxury, comfort, independence, freedom, respect, love, and a three-dollar pantyhose that won't run.

Phyllis Diller

I'd like to have a girl, and I'm saving my money so I can get a good one.

Bob Nickman

Few women care to be laughed at and men not at all, except for large sums of money.

Alan Ayckbourn

A woman must have money and a room of her own if she is to write fiction.

Virginia Woolf

If women didn't exist, all the money in the world would have no meaning.

Aristotle Onassis

Money speaks, but it speaks with a male voice.

Andrea Dworkin

I want a man who's kind and understanding. Is that too much to ask of a millionaire?

Zsa Zsa Gabor

Index

I, J